REBOOTING SRI LANKA

A Comprehensive Plan for Economic Revitalization

Alfonso Borello

Villaggio Publishing Ltd

CONTENTS

INTRODUCTION

Sri Lanka, an island nation situated in the Indian Ocean, has long been known for its rich cultural heritage and scenic beauty. However, in recent years, the country has struggled with economic challenges that have hindered its growth and development. In order to address these challenges, Sri Lanka must adopt bold and innovative strategies that harness the power of technology and international cooperation.

One such strategy is the use of crowdfunding to reboot Sri Lanka's economy. Crowdfunding, which involves raising funds from a large number of individuals through online platforms, has emerged as a viable alternative to traditional lending institutions. It allows entrepreneurs and businesses to access capital from a diverse range of sources, bypassing the often cumbersome and restrictive requirements of banks and other financial institutions.

This approach could be particularly beneficial for Sri Lanka, which has struggled with high levels of debt and limited access to international financing. By embracing crowdfunding, Sri Lanka can tap into a global network of investors and entrepreneurs, while also promoting greater transparency and accountability in the financial sector.

IMF POLICIES AND PRACTICES: CRITICISMS AND CONTROVERSIES

The International Monetary Fund (IMF) is a global organization that was established to promote international monetary cooperation and exchange rate stability. The IMF's primary objective is to ensure the stability of the international monetary system, which includes facilitating the balanced growth of international trade, promoting exchange rate stability, and providing resources to member countries experiencing balance of payments problems.

The IMF provides financial assistance to member countries in need of funds to stabilize their economies and address balance of payments problems. However, the policies and practices of the IMF have been criticized for being biased and for exacerbating economic problems in developing countries. Some of the criticisms include:

Conditionality: The IMF's financial assistance to member countries is often tied to a set of conditions or policy prescriptions, known as conditionality. Critics argue that these conditions are often too rigid and insensitive to the specific needs and circumstances of the borrowing country.

Austerity measures: The IMF has been criticized for imposing harsh austerity measures on borrowing countries as a condition for receiving financial assistance. These measures, which often include deep cuts in public spending and social programs, have been shown to worsen economic conditions and exacerbate poverty in many countries.

Bias towards developed countries: The IMF has been accused of being biased towards developed countries, particularly the United States and Europe. Critics argue that the voting power structure of the IMF disproportionately favors developed countries, and that the policies and practices of the IMF reflect the interests of these countries rather than the needs of the developing world.

Lack of transparency and accountability: The IMF has been criticized for a lack of transparency and accountability in its decision-making processes. Critics argue that the IMF's policies and practices are often opaque and not subject to democratic oversight, which can lead to decisions that are not in the best interests of borrowing countries.

Indeed, the IMF's policies and practices have been the subject of ongoing debate and criticism. While the organization has made efforts to address some of these issues in recent years, there is still a need for greater transparency, accountability, and sensitivity to the specific needs and circumstances of borrowing countries.

GOALS OF THE PLAN

In this discussion, we will explore the potential benefits of using crowdfunding to reboot Sri Lanka's economy, and consider the various challenges and opportunities associated with this approach. We will also examine other innovative strategies, such as the implementation of a digital-only currency and the use of blockchain technology, that could further enhance Sri Lanka's economic potential.

Ultimately, the goal of this discussion is to provide a roadmap for revitalizing Sri Lanka's economy and positioning it for long-term growth and prosperity. By embracing innovative approaches and leveraging the power of technology, Sri Lanka can unlock its full potential and establish itself as a leader in the region.

INVESTMENT IN INFRASTRUCTURE

Investment in infrastructure is a crucial component of any economic revitalization strategy. In Sri Lanka, there is a pressing need for infrastructure development, particularly in areas such as transportation, energy, and telecommunications. To attract investors and facilitate economic growth, Sri Lanka must develop a robust infrastructure that can support business operations and promote connectivity both domestically and internationally.

One potential strategy for infrastructure development is through public-private partnerships (PPPs), which can bring together the resources and expertise of both the public and private sectors. PPPs can help to bridge the financing gap for infrastructure projects, while also ensuring that projects are well-planned, executed efficiently, and benefit the public.

Another potential approach is through the use of innovative financing mechanisms, such as green bonds or social impact bonds. These financing mechanisms can help to attract capital for infrastructure projects that have environmental or social benefits, while also providing financial returns for investors.

Investment in infrastructure not only creates jobs and stimulates economic activity, but also provides the foundation for long-term growth and development. Sri Lanka must prioritize infrastructure investment as a key component of its economic revitalization strategy.

STREAMLINING BUSINESS REGULATIONS

Streamlining business regulations is another important strategy for economic revitalization. In Sri Lanka, businesses face numerous bureaucratic hurdles and cumbersome regulatory requirements that can hinder growth and discourage investment. To attract and retain businesses, Sri Lanka must create a more business-friendly environment that encourages entrepreneurship, innovation, and investment.

One potential approach is through the simplification and digitization of regulatory processes. By digitizing regulatory processes and making them more transparent, Sri Lanka can reduce bureaucracy and improve efficiency. This can also help to reduce the opportunities for corruption and promote greater accountability.

Another potential strategy is through the creation of special economic zones (SEZs) or free trade zones (FTZs) that offer streamlined regulations and tax incentives for businesses. These zones can serve as a hub for innovation and investment, attracting domestic and foreign businesses and promoting job creation.

Streamlining business regulations not only benefits businesses, but also creates a more dynamic and competitive economy. Sri Lanka must prioritize regulatory reform as a key component of its economic revitalization strategy.

PROMOTING ENTREPRENEURSHIP AND INNOVATION

Promoting entrepreneurship and innovation is essential to any economic revitalization strategy. In Sri Lanka, there is a growing need to foster entrepreneurship and innovation to drive economic growth and create job opportunities for the country's young and growing population.

A potential strategy is through the establishment of startup incubators and accelerators, which provide mentoring, funding, and networking opportunities for aspiring entrepreneurs. These programs can help to support the development of innovative and scalable businesses that can contribute to economic growth and job creation.

Another potential approach is through the creation of innovation hubs and clusters, which bring together businesses, universities, and research institutions to collaborate and innovate. These hubs can help to create a supportive ecosystem for innovation and entrepreneurship, attracting talented individuals and businesses and fostering a culture of creativity and innovation.

Promoting entrepreneurship and innovation not only creates jobs and stimulates economic activity, but also helps to develop new industries and technologies that can drive long-term growth and competitiveness. Sri Lanka must prioritize the promotion of entrepreneurship and innovation as a key component of its economic revitalization strategy.

TAX INCENTIVES FOR INVESTORS

Tax incentives for investors can be an effective tool for attracting investment and stimulating economic growth. In Sri Lanka, the government can consider offering tax incentives to both domestic and foreign investors to encourage investment in priority sectors and regions.

One potential approach is through tax holidays or reduced tax rates for certain types of investments or businesses. For example, the government could offer tax breaks to investors who invest in sectors such as renewable energy or infrastructure development. Similarly, tax incentives could be offered to businesses that invest in economically disadvantaged regions or in sectors that have a high potential for job creation.

Another potential strategy is through the creation of tax-free zones, where businesses can operate without paying any taxes. These zones can serve as a magnet for investment, attracting domestic and foreign businesses and promoting job creation.

Tax incentives not only encourage investment and job creation but also stimulate economic activity and promote competitiveness. Sri Lanka must prioritize the creation of tax incentives as a key component of its economic revitalization strategy.

CROWDFUNDING AS AN ALTERNATIVE TO THE WORLD BANK AND IMF

Bypassing the World Bank and IMF could offer several potential benefits for Sri Lanka, including:

1. Independence: Sri Lanka would have greater autonomy in designing and implementing economic policies without external pressure or influence from international organizations.

2. Flexibility: By not being subject to the rigid conditions and guidelines set by the World Bank and IMF, Sri Lanka could have more flexibility in tailoring economic policies to fit its specific needs and circumstances.

3. Reduced Debt Burden: Sri Lanka would not have to rely on loans from the World Bank and IMF, which often come with high-interest rates and strict repayment terms, leading to a reduced debt burden.

4. Promotion of Local Expertise: By bypassing the World Bank and IMF, Sri Lanka could focus on promoting local expertise and talents in designing and implementing economic policies.

5. Increased Public Participation: Crowdfunding initiatives could encourage greater public

participation in the economic development of Sri Lanka, leading to more democratic and inclusive decision-making processes.

However, it's important to note that bypassing the World Bank and IMF could also have potential drawbacks, such as reduced access to global expertise and resources, and potential challenges in accessing international markets and aid programs. It is essential to carefully consider the potential benefits and risks before making any decisions.

IMPLEMENTING A DIGITAL-ONLY CURRENCY FOR GREATER TRANSPARENCY

The use of a digital-only currency to prevent misuse in Sri Lanka could offer several potential benefits, including:

Increased Transparency: A digital-only currency would enable greater transparency and accountability in financial transactions, reducing the risk of misuse and corruption.

Reduced Costs: A digital-only currency could reduce transaction costs and increase efficiency, which would be especially beneficial for small businesses and low-income individuals.

Improved Security: A digital-only currency would be less vulnerable to theft and fraud, as it would be difficult to counterfeit or manipulate.

Inflation Control: A digital-only currency would enable better control of inflation by allowing the central bank to monitor and adjust the money supply more easily.

Financial Inclusion: A digital-only currency would enable greater financial inclusion by providing access to financial services for unbanked and underbanked populations.

However, there are also potential challenges and risks associated with the use of a digital-only currency, including:

Technical Barriers: The adoption of a digital-only currency

would require significant technological infrastructure and resources, which may be challenging to develop and implement.

Cybersecurity Risks: A digital-only currency would be vulnerable to cyber-attacks, which could have significant financial and economic consequences.

Volatility: The value of a digital-only currency could be highly volatile, leading to potential risks for investors and users.

Adoption and Acceptance: The adoption and acceptance of a digital-only currency could be challenging, as it would require significant changes in user behavior and attitudes towards traditional currency.

Overall, the use of a digital-only currency to prevent misuse in Sri Lanka could offer significant potential benefits, but it would also require careful consideration and planning to mitigate potential risks and challenges.

IMPLEMENTING TRANSPARENT ACCOUNTING PRACTICES

Accounting practices are critical for ensuring financial transparency, accountability, and credibility in Sri Lanka. Here are some considerations for accounting practices in the country:

Adoption of International Accounting Standards: Sri Lanka has already adopted some international accounting standards, but further adoption and adherence to these standards could improve financial transparency and accountability.

Improved Financial Reporting: Financial reporting should be more detailed, timely, and accessible to the public, which could increase the confidence of investors and other stakeholders.

Strengthening Audit Functions: Auditing should be more rigorous, independent, and transparent, with stricter standards and penalties for noncompliance.

Enhancing Corporate Governance: Corporate governance standards should be strengthened to promote more transparent and ethical business practices, such as greater board independence and more effective risk management.

Encouraging Public Participation: Encouraging public participation in the auditing and reporting processes could increase accountability and transparency.

Encouraging Digitalization: Digitalizing accounting practices could improve efficiency and accuracy, reduce opportunities for fraud, and provide better access to financial information.

Training and Capacity Building: Training and capacity building programs should be developed to enhance the skills and expertise of accounting professionals and improve compliance with accounting standards.

Overall, implementing strong accounting practices in Sri Lanka is critical for maintaining financial stability and promoting economic growth. By adhering to international accounting standards, enhancing financial reporting and auditing, improving corporate governance, encouraging public participation, promoting digitalization, and investing in training and capacity building, Sri Lanka can strengthen its financial infrastructure and increase its attractiveness to investors.

DEVELOPING A ROBUST FINANCIAL REPORTING SYSTEM

Developing a robust financial reporting system is essential to any economic revitalization strategy. In Sri Lanka, there is a need to improve financial reporting standards to attract more investment and promote transparency and accountability.

One potential strategy is through the implementation of International Financial Reporting Standards (IFRS), which can enhance the quality of financial reporting and provide more accurate and comparable financial information to investors. By adopting IFRS, Sri Lanka can align its financial reporting standards with global best practices and attract more foreign investment.

Another potential approach is through the strengthening of corporate governance practices, which can promote transparency and accountability in financial reporting. This includes the establishment of independent audit committees and the adoption of robust internal control systems to prevent fraudulent financial reporting.

Developing a robust financial reporting system not only attracts investment but also promotes accountability and transparency, ensuring that public resources are being used effectively and efficiently. Sri Lanka must prioritize the development of a robust financial reporting system as a key component of its economic revitalization strategy.

IMPLEMENTING MEASURES
TO PREVENT FRAUD
AND CORRUPTION

Preventing fraud and corruption is essential to any economic revitalization strategy. In Sri Lanka, there is a need to implement measures to prevent fraud and corruption in financial reporting to attract more investment and promote transparency and accountability.

One potential strategy is through the establishment of an independent regulatory body to oversee financial reporting practices and prevent fraudulent financial reporting. This body can have the power to investigate and penalize any individual or organization found guilty of fraudulent financial reporting practices.

Another potential approach is through the implementation of anti-corruption measures, such as the establishment of a code of conduct for public officials and the creation of an independent anti-corruption agency. These measures can promote transparency and accountability in the public sector, ensuring that public resources are being used effectively and efficiently.

Implementing measures to prevent fraud and corruption not only attracts investment but also promotes accountability and transparency, ensuring that public resources are being used for the betterment of the country. Sri Lanka must prioritize the implementation of measures to prevent fraud and corruption as a key component of its economic revitalization strategy.

OPEN BORDERS

Open borders can potentially help to increase investments in Sri Lanka in several ways:

Increased Movement of Capital: Open borders could facilitate the movement of capital, enabling investors to bring in funds more easily and efficiently, which could stimulate economic growth and development.

Attracting Foreign Investment: Open borders could attract more foreign investment by creating a more welcoming and investor-friendly environment, which could create jobs and generate income for Sri Lanka.

Promoting Knowledge and Technology Transfer: Open borders could enable the transfer of knowledge, technology, and skills from foreign investors to Sri Lankan businesses, improving competitiveness and innovation.

Encouraging Trade: Open borders could encourage more trade and commerce with neighboring countries, increasing Sri Lanka's economic integration with the region.

However, it's important to note that open borders could also have potential drawbacks and challenges, including:

Security Concerns: Open borders could increase the risk of illegal immigration, smuggling, and trafficking, which could pose security challenges for Sri Lanka.

Competition for Local Businesses: Open borders could increase competition for local businesses, potentially leading to a displacement of small and medium-sized enterprises.

Cultural Differences: Open borders could result in cultural clashes and social tensions, which could negatively impact social cohesion and integration.

Pressure on Infrastructure: Open borders could increase the pressure on Sri Lanka's infrastructure, such as transportation, healthcare, and education systems.

Therefore, it's essential to carefully consider the potential benefits and risks of open borders before making any decisions, and to implement policies and measures to address any potential challenges that may arise.

ENCOURAGING FOREIGN INVESTMENT THROUGH OPEN BORDERS

Encouraging foreign investment is essential to any economic revitalization strategy. In Sri Lanka, there is a need to open borders and create a more favorable environment for foreign investors to invest in the country.

One potential strategy is through the relaxation of visa requirements for foreign investors and entrepreneurs, making it easier for them to enter and exit the country. This can encourage more foreign investment and promote entrepreneurship, leading to job creation and economic growth.

Another potential approach is through the establishment of special economic zones, which can offer tax incentives and other benefits to foreign investors. These zones can create a more attractive environment for investment and promote the development of new industries in Sri Lanka.

Encouraging foreign investment through open borders not only attracts investment but also promotes economic growth and job creation. Sri Lanka must prioritize the relaxation of visa requirements and the establishment of special economic zones as a key component of its economic revitalization strategy.

PROVIDING VISA AND IMMIGRATION INCENTIVES FOR INVESTORS

To encourage foreign investment in Sri Lanka, it is essential to provide visa and immigration incentives to potential investors. This can create a more attractive environment for foreign investment and promote economic growth in the country.

One potential strategy is through the establishment of a streamlined visa and immigration process for foreign investors. This can include fast-tracked visas and work permits, as well as providing residency options for investors and their families.

Another potential approach is through the creation of special visa categories for investors, entrepreneurs, and skilled workers. This can attract more talent and investment to Sri Lanka, leading to the development of new industries and job creation.

Providing visa and immigration incentives for investors not only attracts investment but also promotes economic growth and job creation. Sri Lanka must prioritize the establishment of a streamlined visa and immigration process and the creation of special visa categories as a key component of its economic revitalization strategy.

POTENTIAL CONSIDERATION OF A DIGITAL ONLY CURRENCY

The use of a digital-only currency in Sri Lanka could offer several potential benefits, including:

Increased Transparency: A digital-only currency would enable greater transparency and accountability in financial transactions, reducing the risk of misuse and corruption.

Reduced Costs: A digital-only currency could reduce transaction costs and increase efficiency, which would be especially beneficial for small businesses and low-income individuals.

Improved Security: A digital-only currency would be less vulnerable to theft and fraud, as it would be difficult to counterfeit or manipulate.

Inflation Control: A digital-only currency would enable better control of inflation by allowing the central bank to monitor and adjust the money supply more easily.

Financial Inclusion: A digital-only currency would enable greater financial inclusion by providing access to financial services for unbanked and underbanked populations.

However, there are also potential challenges and risks associated with the use of a digital-only currency, including:

Technical Barriers: The adoption of a digital-only currency

would require significant technological infrastructure and resources, which may be challenging to develop and implement.

Cybersecurity Risks: A digital-only currency would be vulnerable to cyber-attacks, which could have significant financial and economic consequences.

Volatility: The value of a digital-only currency could be highly volatile, leading to potential risks for investors and users.

Adoption and Acceptance: The adoption and acceptance of a digital-only currency could be challenging, as it would require significant changes in user behavior and attitudes towards traditional currency.

Indeed, the use of a digital-only currency to prevent misuse in Sri Lanka could offer significant potential benefits, but it would also require careful consideration and planning to mitigate potential risks and challenges.

EVALUATING BLOCKCHAIN TECHNOLOGY AS A VIABLE OPTION

Blockchain technology is a viable option for improving transparency, security, and accountability in various industries, including finance and supply chain management. However, whether it is the best option for Sri Lanka would depend on several factors.

Here are some considerations to keep in mind when deciding whether to use blockchain technology:

Complexity and Cost: Blockchain technology can be complex and expensive to implement, especially for small and medium-sized enterprises. It is important to assess the costs and benefits of using blockchain technology compared to alternative solutions.

Scalability: Blockchain technology has scalability limitations, which can be a challenge when implementing it on a large scale. For Sri Lanka, it would be essential to evaluate whether blockchain technology can meet the needs of its growing economy and population.

Regulatory Framework: Blockchain technology is still a relatively new concept, and regulatory frameworks for its use may not be fully established. It is important to ensure that any blockchain-based solutions are compliant with relevant regulations and standards.

Adoption and Integration: Blockchain technology requires a certain level of technical expertise and understanding to implement and use effectively. It is important to assess whether there is enough local expertise and support for blockchain technology in Sri Lanka.

Interoperability: Blockchain technology can be incompatible with existing systems and technologies, which can be a challenge when integrating it with legacy systems. It is important to ensure that any blockchain-based solutions are interoperable with existing systems and technologies.

Overall, blockchain technology can be a viable option for Sri Lanka, but it is essential to carefully evaluate the benefits and challenges of using blockchain technology compared to alternative solutions. Additionally, it is important to assess whether the local ecosystem in Sri Lanka is ready for the adoption and implementation of blockchain technology.

BLOCKCHAIN IN PLAIN ENGLISH

Blockchain is a digital ledger that is used to record transactions between two parties in a secure and transparent manner. It's called a "blockchain" because transactions are recorded in blocks, and each block is linked to the previous one, creating a chain of blocks.

In a blockchain, each transaction is verified and recorded by multiple parties in the network, rather than by a single central authority. This creates a level of security and trust in the system, as all participants in the network can see and verify the transactions.

The data stored in a blockchain is immutable, meaning it cannot be altered or deleted once it has been recorded. This ensures that the information in the blockchain is accurate and tamper-proof.

Blockchains are used for a variety of applications, including cryptocurrencies, supply chain management, and digital identity verification. They have the potential to revolutionize industries and create new business models by enabling secure and transparent transactions without the need for intermediaries.

EXPLORING ALTERNATIVE TECHNOLOGIES

There are several alternatives to blockchain technology that can be considered for improving transparency, security, and accountability in Sri Lanka, depending on the specific use case and requirements. Here are some examples:

Distributed Ledger Technology (DLT): DLT is similar to blockchain technology, but it uses different consensus mechanisms and does not require mining. DLT can be more scalable and energy-efficient than blockchain technology, and it can be used for various applications, such as supply chain management and digital identity.

Traditional Databases: Traditional databases can be a viable alternative to blockchain technology for some applications, such as financial transactions and record-keeping. Databases can be more efficient and cost-effective than blockchain technology, especially for small and medium-sized businesses.

Federated Byzantine Agreement (FBA): FBA is a consensus mechanism that can be used to ensure agreement among nodes in a network. FBA can be more efficient and scalable than traditional blockchain technology, and it can be used for various applications, such as financial transactions and asset management.

Multi-Signature Technology: Multi-signature technology can be used to enhance security and accountability in financial transactions by requiring multiple parties to approve a transaction. Multi-signature technology can be implemented on traditional databases or other distributed ledger technologies.

Open Banking: Open banking is a banking model that allows third-party developers to build applications and services around banks' APIs. Open banking can improve transparency, security, and competition in the financial industry, and it can be a viable alternative to blockchain technology for some applications.

In summary, there are several alternatives to blockchain technology that can be considered for improving transparency, security, and accountability in Sri Lanka, depending on the specific use case and requirements. It is important to carefully evaluate the benefits and drawbacks of each alternative before making a decision.

DISTRIBUTED LEDGER TECHNOLOGY (DLT) EXPLAINED

Distributed Ledger Technology (DLT) is a system for recording and verifying transactions in a decentralized and secure manner. DLT is a broader term that encompasses various types of digital ledgers, including blockchain.

In a DLT system, data is stored across a network of computers, rather than on a single centralized server. Each computer, or node, in the network has a copy of the ledger, and any changes made to the ledger are recorded and verified by multiple nodes. This ensures that the data is secure, transparent, and tamper-proof.

DLT can be used in a variety of applications, such as supply chain management, digital identity verification, and financial transactions. It offers a more secure and efficient way of recording and verifying data, as there is no central point of failure or control.

One of the main benefits of DLT is that it can reduce the need for intermediaries, such as banks or other financial institutions, by enabling direct transactions between parties. This can lower transaction costs and increase efficiency in various industries.

Indeed, DLT is a powerful technology with the potential to transform the way we store and verify data. It offers a secure, decentralized, and transparent way of recording transactions, making it an attractive option for businesses and organizations seeking to improve their operations and reduce costs.

TRADITIONAL DATABASES EXPLAINED

Traditional databases are computer systems used to store, organize, and manage data. They are used in a wide range of applications, from financial institutions to social media platforms to e-commerce websites.

In a traditional database system, data is stored in tables consisting of rows and columns, and relationships between the tables are defined by the use of keys. The database is managed by a database management system (DBMS), which provides tools for creating, modifying, and querying the data.

One of the main advantages of traditional databases is that they offer high performance and scalability. They are designed to handle large volumes of data and support multiple users accessing the database simultaneously.

Another advantage is that traditional databases provide a high degree of flexibility in terms of data storage and retrieval. They allow for complex queries and data manipulation, and can be easily integrated with other applications.

However, traditional databases have some limitations. They are typically centralized, meaning that all data is stored on a single server, making them vulnerable to security breaches and system failures. They can also be expensive to set up and maintain, and may require specialized skills to manage.

Overall, traditional databases are a widely used technology that offer many benefits in terms of data storage, retrieval, and manipulation. However, they may not be the best option for all use cases, particularly those that require a high degree of decentralization and security.

FEDERATED BYZANTINE AGREEMENT (FBA) EXPLAINED

Federated Byzantine Agreement (FBA) is a consensus algorithm used in distributed systems to achieve agreement among a group of nodes about the state of a system. It is based on the Byzantine fault-tolerant (BFT) consensus algorithm, which allows a group of nodes to reach consensus even in the presence of failures or malicious actors.

In FBA, nodes are organized into a network of federated sub-networks, with each sub-network having its own set of validators. Each validator maintains a copy of the ledger and can approve or reject transactions. The sub-networks communicate with each other to reach consensus on the state of the system.

FBA uses a voting process to reach consensus on the validity of transactions. When a transaction is submitted, it is broadcast to all validators in the sub-network. Each validator independently checks the transaction for validity, and then votes on whether to approve or reject it. If a supermajority of validators in a sub-network approve the transaction, it is considered valid and added to the ledger.

One of the benefits of FBA is its scalability, as it can handle large numbers of validators without sacrificing performance. It also allows for greater decentralization than traditional consensus algorithms, as nodes can join or leave the network without disrupting consensus.

However, FBA is not without its challenges. It requires a high degree of coordination among validators and can be vulnerable to attacks from malicious actors. Additionally, there can be difficulties in managing the network and determining who should be allowed to participate as a validator.

Overall, FBA is a promising consensus algorithm for distributed systems, particularly in cases where decentralization and scalability are important. Its ability to achieve consensus even in the presence of failures or malicious actors makes it a valuable tool for achieving trust in decentralized systems.

MULTI-SIGNATURE TECHNOLOGY EXPLAINED

Multi-Signature (Multi-Sig) technology is a security feature used in digital transactions and cryptocurrency wallets. It requires the approval of multiple parties before a transaction can be executed, making it more secure than a single signature.

In a multi-signature system, a transaction must be signed by a predetermined number of parties, typically two or more, in order to be executed. Each party involved has their own unique private key, which is used to sign the transaction. When a transaction is initiated, it is sent to all parties involved, who then must approve it with their own private key. Once the required number of approvals has been reached, the transaction is executed and recorded on the blockchain.

This technology is particularly useful in situations where high-value transactions are involved or where multiple parties are involved in managing funds. For example, in a business setting, a multi-signature wallet could require the approval of several executives before a large payment is made. In a personal setting, a multi-signature wallet could require the approval of multiple family members before a significant amount of cryptocurrency is transferred.

Multi-signature technology provides an additional layer of security to digital transactions by requiring multiple parties to approve a transaction. This can help prevent fraud, theft, and hacking attempts. It is a valuable tool for those who prioritize security and wish to reduce the risk of unauthorized access to their digital assets.

OPEN BANKING EXPLAINED

Open banking is a system in which banks and financial institutions allow third-party developers to access their customer data and payment infrastructure through open APIs (application programming interfaces). This enables developers to create new financial applications and services that can improve the customer experience and promote innovation in the financial industry.

With open banking, customers can securely share their financial data with authorized third-party providers, such as budgeting and savings apps, investment management services, and lending platforms. These providers can then use the data to create personalized services and financial products tailored to the needs of individual customers. For example, a budgeting app might use a customer's transaction history to provide personalized spending recommendations, while an investment platform might use a customer's financial data to create a customized investment portfolio.

Open banking also enables customers to initiate payments directly from their bank accounts through third-party payment providers, without the need for a credit or debit card. This can simplify the payment process and reduce the risk of fraud, as the payment is made directly from the customer's bank account.

In addition to improving the customer experience and promoting innovation, open banking can also increase competition in the financial industry. By enabling third-party providers to access customer data and payment infrastructure, new players can enter the market and compete with traditional banks, driving down costs and improving services for customers.

Indeed, open banking represents a significant shift in the financial industry towards greater transparency, collaboration, and innovation. While there are potential risks associated with open banking, such as data privacy concerns and increased competition for traditional banks, the benefits for customers and the industry as a whole are significant.

SUMMARY OF THE PLAN

In summary, this plan proposes a comprehensive approach to rebooting Sri Lanka's economy through crowdfunding, investment in infrastructure, streamlining business regulations, promoting entrepreneurship and innovation, tax incentives for investors, implementing robust financial reporting systems, preventing fraud and corruption, providing visa and immigration incentives for investors, evaluating emerging technologies like blockchain, and exploring simpler options like APIs, mobile banking, cloud computing, digital payments, and other technologies. By implementing these measures, Sri Lanka can attract foreign investment, create jobs, and promote economic growth. It is important to note that this plan is not exhaustive and should be adapted to the specific needs and context of Sri Lanka. However, by following these guidelines, Sri Lanka can move towards a more prosperous and sustainable future.

IMPORTANCE OF COLLABORATION BETWEEN THE GOVERNMENT, PRIVATE SECTOR, AND THE COMMUNITY

In conclusion, it is important to emphasize the critical role of collaboration between the government, private sector, and the community in implementing this plan. This is not a task that can be accomplished by any one entity alone. Rather, it requires a collective effort and a shared commitment to the economic development of Sri Lanka. It is also important to prioritize transparency, accountability, and inclusivity throughout the process, to ensure that all stakeholders have a voice and that the benefits of economic growth are distributed fairly. By working together, Sri Lanka can leverage the power of crowdfunding, innovation, and emerging technologies to create a brighter future for all its citizens.

THE BUSINESS PLAN OUTLINE

The following is a hypothetical business model that could be considered as a starting point.

I. Executive Summary

• An overview of the crowdfunding platform
• Highlight of the key features and benefits for donors and project organizers
• Summary the potential impact on Sri Lanka's economy and society

II. Market Analysis

• Analysis the current crowdfunding market in Sri Lanka
• Gaps and opportunities for a new crowdfunding platform
• SWOT analysis to assess the strengths, weaknesses, opportunities, and threats

III. Business Model

• Outline of the revenue streams and pricing strategy
• How the platform will generate revenue while maintaining transparency and fairness
• Projections for the platform's financial performance

IV. Marketing and Communication Strategy

• Developing a marketing and communication strategy to reach potential donors and project organizers
• Key channels and tactics for promoting the platform
• Budget and timeline for the marketing and communication activities

V. Platform Features and Functionality

- Outline of the key features and functionality of the platform, including payment processing, project management, and reporting
- How the platform will ensure transparency and accountability for funds raised and disbursed
- A roadmap for future development and enhancement of the platform

VI. Team and Operations

- Introducing the team responsible for the development and operation of the platform
- Outline of the organizational structure and roles and responsibilities of the team members
- How the platform will be managed and maintained over time

VII. Risk Management

- Potential risks and challenges associated with the platform
- A risk management strategy to mitigate and manage these risks
- Contingency plan for unforeseen events or issues

VIII. Conclusion

- Summary of the key points of the business plan
- Highlight of the potential impact of the platform on Sri Lanka's economy and society
- Encouraging potential investors and partners to support the platform's development and launch.

I. EXECUTIVE SUMMARY

AN OVERVIEW OF THE CROWDFUNDING PLATFORM

The crowdfunding platform proposed in this plan aims to revitalize the economy of Sri Lanka through alternative financing options. By harnessing the power of the internet and social networks, this platform will connect local entrepreneurs and businesses with a global community of investors, allowing them to raise funds for their projects in a transparent and efficient manner.

The platform will prioritize projects that align with Sri Lanka's economic development goals, including infrastructure development, entrepreneurship and innovation, and sustainable tourism. It will also provide support and resources to project owners to help them create compelling campaigns and attract investors.

This crowdfunding platform will be complemented by a range of economic revitalization measures, including tax incentives for investors, streamlining business regulations, and promoting entrepreneurship and innovation. By working together, these measures will create an environment that fosters economic growth and development in Sri Lanka.

In brief, this platform will help to bypass traditional financing options such as the World Bank and IMF, and provide a more accessible and sustainable way for Sri Lanka to finance its economic development goals.

HIGHLIGHT OF THE KEY FEATURES AND BENEFITS FOR DONORS AND PROJECT ORGANIZERS

The crowdfunding platform proposed in this plan offers a range of key features and benefits for both donors and project organizers.

For project organizers, the platform provides a streamlined and accessible way to raise funds for their projects. They can create compelling campaigns and attract a global community of investors through the power of the internet and social networks. The platform also offers resources and support to help project organizers create successful campaigns.

For donors, the platform offers a transparent and efficient way to support projects that align with Sri Lanka's economic development goals. They can browse and select from a range of projects, and track the progress of their donations in real-time. By using the platform, donors can be confident that their contributions are making a tangible difference in the development of Sri Lanka.

Overall, this crowdfunding platform offers a range of benefits for both project organizers and donors, including accessibility, transparency, and efficiency. It provides a powerful tool for driving economic growth and development in Sri Lanka, while also connecting local communities with a global network of supporters.

SUMMARY OF THE POTENTIAL IMPACT ON SRI LANKA'S ECONOMY AND SOCIETY

The crowdfunding platform outlined in this plan has the potential to significantly impact Sri Lanka's economy and society. By providing a means for individuals and organizations to raise funds for their projects, the platform can stimulate entrepreneurship and innovation, promote job creation, and revitalize the economy. It also has the potential to promote social and environmental initiatives that can benefit communities across the country. By leveraging the power of technology and community engagement, the crowdfunding platform can create a more inclusive and vibrant economy that benefits all Sri Lankans.

II. MARKET ANALYSIS

ANALYSIS OF THE CURRENT CROWDFUNDING MARKET IN SRI LANKA

The current crowdfunding market in Sri Lanka is relatively underdeveloped, with few platforms available for project organizers to raise funds. However, there is a growing interest in crowdfunding among entrepreneurs, social activists, and creative professionals. The lack of access to traditional funding sources and the desire to reach a wider audience are some of the key drivers of this interest. While the market is still in its early stages, there is a significant potential for growth, particularly in areas such as education, healthcare, environmental sustainability, and social entrepreneurship. The emergence of new technologies and the increasing use of social media platforms are also likely to contribute to the growth of the crowdfunding market in Sri Lanka.

GAPS AND OPPORTUNITIES FOR A NEW CROWDFUNDING PLATFORM

A market analysis of the current crowdfunding landscape in Sri Lanka has revealed several gaps and opportunities for a new platform. While there are a few existing platforms in the country, they are limited in scope and primarily focus on charity and social causes. There is a significant lack of crowdfunding platforms that cater to small businesses and startups seeking funding. Additionally, the current platforms are not user-friendly and lack transparency in the disbursement of funds. This presents an opportunity for a new crowdfunding platform that can offer a more streamlined, transparent, and user-friendly experience for donors and project organizers alike.

SWOT ANALYSIS TO ASSESS THE STRENGTHS, WEAKNESSES, OPPORTUNITIES, AND THREATS

A SWOT analysis can be conducted to assess the strengths, weaknesses, opportunities, and threats of the proposed crowdfunding platform in Sri Lanka.

Strengths:

1. There is a growing interest in crowdfunding in Sri Lanka, indicating a potential market for a new platform.
2. Crowdfunding provides an alternative source of financing for projects that may not be able to access traditional financing options.
3. A crowdfunding platform can create a sense of community and engagement among donors and project organizers.

Weaknesses:

1. Crowdfunding is a relatively new concept in Sri Lanka and may not yet be fully understood by potential users.
2. The lack of trust and security in online transactions may discourage some donors from

contributing to projects on the platform.

3. There may be a limited pool of potential donors and project organizers in Sri Lanka, which could limit the growth potential of the platform.

Opportunities:

1. There is a need for more financing options for small businesses and startups in Sri Lanka, which could be addressed by a crowdfunding platform.
2. The platform can attract donations from the Sri Lankan diaspora and other international donors, increasing the potential pool of funds available for projects.
3. The platform can provide a transparent and accountable way for donors to track the progress of projects they have contributed to.

Threats:

1. There may be competition from existing crowdfunding platforms in Sri Lanka or other countries.
2. Economic and political instability in Sri Lanka could discourage donors from investing in projects on the platform.
3. The lack of regulations and legal framework for crowdfunding in Sri Lanka could create uncertainty for the platform and its users.

III. BUSINESS MODEL

OUTLINE OF THE REVENUE STREAMS AND PRICING STRATEGY

The revenue streams for the crowdfunding platform will include fees charged to project organizers for listing their projects, as well as a percentage of the funds raised. The pricing strategy will be based on a tiered approach, with different fees and commission rates depending on the size and complexity of the project. Additionally, the platform may offer premium services for project organizers, such as marketing and promotional support, for an additional fee. The pricing strategy will be designed to be competitive with other crowdfunding platforms in the market while also generating sustainable revenue for the platform's operations and growth.

HOW THE PLATFORM WILL GENERATE REVENUE WHILE MAINTAINING TRANSPARENCY AND FAIRNESS

To generate revenue, the platform will take a percentage of the funds raised by the project organizers. This percentage can vary based on the type and size of the project. However, transparency and fairness will be maintained by setting clear and consistent pricing policies for all projects, and by disclosing all fees and charges to both donors and project organizers.

Additionally, the platform may explore alternative revenue streams such as offering premium features and services to project organizers for a fee, or through partnerships with businesses or organizations that align with the platform's values and mission. The platform will also strive to maintain low operational costs to maximize the impact of the funds raised.

PROJECTIONS FOR THE PLATFORM'S FINANCIAL PERFORMANCE

To provide an understanding of the potential financial performance of the crowdfunding platform, we have developed a set of projections for the first three years of operation. Our projections are based on conservative estimates and assume a gradual increase in platform usage over time.

We anticipate generating revenue through a percentage-based fee structure for successful fundraising campaigns, as well as offering premium services such as marketing and project management support for a fee. Our pricing strategy is designed to be competitive with existing platforms in Sri Lanka while also reflecting the added value of our platform's unique features and benefits.

Based on our projections, we anticipate generating a revenue of LKR X in the first year, LKR Y in the second year, and LKR Z in the third year. Our financial projections take into account the costs of platform development, marketing, and ongoing maintenance, as well as potential risks and uncertainties. We believe that our revenue projections are achievable and that the crowdfunding platform has the potential to become a financially sustainable and impactful venture.

IV. MARKETING AND COMMUNICATION STRATEGY

DEVELOPING A MARKETING AND COMMUNICATION STRATEGY TO REACH POTENTIAL DONORS AND PROJECT ORGANIZERS

A comprehensive marketing and communication strategy is essential for the success of a crowdfunding platform. The following key points should be considered:

Target audience: Identify the target audience for the platform and understand their needs and preferences.

Branding: Develop a strong and recognizable brand for the platform that resonates with the target audience.

Communication channels: Identify the most effective communication channels to reach the target audience, such as social media, email marketing, and advertising.

Content strategy: Develop a content strategy that provides valuable information to potential donors and project organizers. This could include blog posts, case studies, and success stories.

Influencer marketing: Collaborate with influencers in the relevant industries or communities to reach a wider audience.

Events: Organize events to showcase successful projects and engage with potential donors and project organizers.

Partnerships: Form partnerships with relevant organizations, such as NGOs and local governments, to expand the reach of the platform and provide additional resources to project organizers.

By developing a comprehensive marketing and communication strategy, the crowdfunding platform can effectively reach its target audience and drive engagement and growth.

KEY CHANNELS AND TACTICS FOR PROMOTING THE PLATFORM

Some potential key channels and tactics for promoting the crowdfunding platform may include:

Social media marketing: Utilizing popular social media platforms such as Facebook, Twitter, LinkedIn, and Instagram to reach a wider audience and promote the platform.

Influencer marketing: Partnering with influential individuals or organizations in Sri Lanka who can promote the platform to their followers and networks.

Email marketing: Creating email campaigns to target potential donors and project organizers and keep them informed about new projects and updates.

Content marketing: Developing high-quality content such as blog posts, videos, and infographics that provide value to potential users and position the platform as a trusted resource.

Events and partnerships: Hosting events or partnering with organizations and institutions to raise awareness about the platform and its impact on Sri Lanka.

Public relations: Working with media outlets to secure coverage and interviews about the platform and its mission.

The specific channels and tactics used will depend on the target audience and budget of the crowdfunding platform. A well-designed and executed marketing and communication strategy will be critical to the success of the platform.

BUDGET AND TIMELINE FOR THE MARKETING AND COMMUNICATION ACTIVITIES

Here's an example of what the section on budget and timeline for marketing and communication activities might look like:

Budget and Timeline

To successfully launch and promote the crowdfunding platform, a marketing and communication budget of LKR 5 million will be allocated for the first year. This budget will cover the costs of advertising, public relations, social media, and event marketing. The budget will be allocated as follows:

Advertising: LKR X million
Public Relations: LKR X million
Social Media: LKR X million
Event Marketing: LKR X million

The following is a tentative timeline for the marketing and communication activities:

Pre-Launch (3 months prior to launch): Develop branding, messaging, and a social media strategy. Begin outreach to key influencers, media outlets, and potential donors and project organizers.

Launch (1 month): Host a launch event and press conference to introduce the platform to the public. Implement targeted advertising and social media campaigns to reach potential users.

First Quarter (3 months after launch): Continue to execute advertising and social media campaigns. Host workshops and events to educate potential users on how to use the platform. Publish press releases and engage with media outlets to promote the platform.

Second Quarter (6 months after launch): Review the marketing and communication strategy and make any necessary adjustments. Continue to engage with potential users and stakeholders through events, workshops, and social media. Consider partnerships with organizations that align with the platform's values and mission.

Third Quarter (9 months after launch): Focus on engaging with existing users and encouraging them to spread the word about the platform. Implement referral programs and incentives for users who successfully fund or launch a project. Consider sponsorships and collaborations with local businesses to expand the platform's reach.

Fourth Quarter (12 months after launch): Conduct a comprehensive review of the marketing and communication strategy and assess the platform's growth and impact. Based on the results, adjust the budget and strategy for the following year.

V. PLATFORM FEATURES AND FUNCTIONALITY

OUTLINE OF THE KEY FEATURES AND FUNCTIONALITY OF THE PLATFORM, INCLUDING PAYMENT PROCESSING, PROJECT MANAGEMENT, AND REPORTING

The crowdfunding platform will have several key features and functionalities to facilitate the donation process and project management. These include:

Payment Processing: The platform will integrate with a secure payment gateway to allow donors to contribute funds using their preferred payment method, including credit/debit cards, bank transfers, and mobile payments.

Project Management: Project organizers can create a profile and submit their project proposal for review. The platform will provide tools for organizers to manage their project, including setting funding goals, updating donors on the project's progress, and tracking donations.

Reporting: The platform will provide real-time reporting on the status of each project, including the total amount of funds raised, donor information, and project milestones achieved.

Feedback and Reviews: Donors can provide feedback and

reviews of the project and the platform, helping to build trust and credibility.

Social Sharing: The platform will have social sharing features to allow donors to share projects on social media, increasing their visibility and reach.

These features will enable a seamless and transparent donation process while providing project organizers with the tools they need to manage their project effectively.

HOW THE PLATFORM WILL ENSURE TRANSPARENCY AND ACCOUNTABILITY FOR FUNDS RAISED AND DISBURSED

To ensure transparency and accountability, the platform will have features such as real-time reporting, project tracking, and regular updates from project organizers. The platform will also implement secure payment processing to prevent fraudulent activities, with funds being held in escrow until the project reaches its funding target. The platform will also have a system for dispute resolution and a clear refund policy in case the project fails to deliver as promised. These features and policies will help build trust among donors and project organizers, and ensure that funds are used as intended.

A ROADMAP FOR FUTURE DEVELOPMENT AND ENHANCEMENT OF THE PLATFORM

To enhance the platform's functionality and usability, the following features will be developed:

Social sharing: The platform will allow donors and project organizers to share campaign pages on social media platforms to increase visibility and engagement.

Mobile app: The platform will develop a mobile app to allow donors and project organizers to access the platform's features and functionality on-the-go.

AI-powered recommendation engine: The platform will use machine learning algorithms to suggest projects to donors based on their interests and donation history. This will help donors discover new and relevant projects to support and increase engagement on the platform.

Integration with blockchain technology: The platform will explore the use of blockchain technology to ensure the security and immutability of transaction records and increase trust in the platform.

The crowdfunding platform will prioritize the continuous improvement and development of its features and functionality to meet the evolving needs of its users and provide the best possible experience for donors and project organizers.

VI. TEAM AND OPERATIONS

INTRODUCING THE TEAM RESPONSIBLE FOR THE DEVELOPMENT AND OPERATION OF THE PLATFORM

[Insert names and roles of team members]

Our team has extensive experience in the fields of finance, technology, and project management. We are committed to ensuring the success of the platform and delivering tangible benefits to donors, project organizers, and the wider community.

In addition to our core team, we will also be partnering with trusted service providers to ensure seamless and secure operations, including payment processing and data management.

OUTLINE OF THE ORGANIZATIONAL STRUCTURE AND ROLES AND RESPONSIBILITIES OF THE TEAM MEMBERS

- Founder and CEO
- CTO
- COO
- Head of Marketing and Communications
- Head of Finance and Accounting
- Project Manager
- Customer Support Lead

ORGANIZATIONAL STRUCTURE AND ROLES AND RESPONSIBILITIES

- Founder and CEO: Overall strategy and vision, fundraising, external partnerships and relationships
- CTO: Technical development and management of the platform, cybersecurity
- COO: Operations and logistics, internal team management
- Head of Marketing and Communications: Marketing and communication strategy, branding, outreach to potential donors and project organizers
- Head of Finance and Accounting: Financial management, accounting, reporting
- Project Manager: Project management, oversight of project applications and approvals, communication with project organizers
- Customer Support Lead: Customer service and support, technical support for users

KEY PARTNERSHIPS
AND SUPPLIERS

- Payment processors
- Legal and accounting firms
- Hosting and cloud computing providers
- Marketing and advertising agencies (if applicable)

PLANS FOR SCALING OPERATIONS AND HIRING ADDITIONAL TEAM MEMBERS

- Timeline for expansion and growth
- Roles and responsibilities for future hires

HOW THE PLATFORM WILL BE MANAGED AND MAINTAINED OVER TIME

The platform will be managed and maintained by a dedicated team responsible for overseeing the day-to-day operations and ensuring the platform is running smoothly. This team will be composed of individuals with expertise in areas such as technology development, project management, finance, and customer service. Regular maintenance and updates will be performed to ensure that the platform remains secure, reliable, and up-to-date with the latest technologies and best practices. Additionally, the team will be responsible for monitoring project activity, resolving any issues that arise, and communicating with donors and project organizers to ensure a positive user experience.

VII. RISK MANAGEMENT

POTENTIAL RISKS AND CHALLENGES ASSOCIATED WITH THE PLATFORM

Some potential risks and challenges associated with the crowdfunding platform could include:

Fraudulent activities: There is a risk that fraudulent activities may occur on the platform, such as project organizers misusing funds or donors misrepresenting their identities. To mitigate this risk, the platform should implement robust security and verification measures, such as two-factor authentication and Know Your Customer (KYC) protocols.

Lack of funding: There is a risk that the platform may not receive enough donations or projects to sustain its operations. To mitigate this risk, the platform should conduct thorough market research and engage in targeted marketing and outreach efforts to attract potential donors and project organizers.

Reputation management: There is a risk that negative publicity or reviews could damage the platform's reputation and discourage users from participating. To mitigate this risk, the platform should prioritize transparency and communication with users, and establish protocols for addressing and resolving any issues or complaints.

Regulatory compliance: There may be regulatory requirements and compliance issues that the platform needs to address, such as data privacy regulations or financial reporting requirements. To mitigate this risk, the platform should consult with legal and regulatory experts and implement appropriate policies and procedures to ensure compliance.

Technological issues: There is a risk of technical problems or system failures that could impact the platform's operations and reputation. To mitigate this risk, the platform should invest in robust technology infrastructure and conduct regular testing and maintenance to identify and address any issues proactively.

A RISK MANAGEMENT STRATEGY TO MITIGATE AND MANAGE THESE RISKS

The risk management strategy for the crowdfunding platform should include several key components:

Compliance: Ensure compliance with all relevant laws and regulations governing crowdfunding activities in Sri Lanka. This includes setting up appropriate legal and regulatory frameworks, obtaining necessary licenses and permits, and adhering to disclosure and reporting requirements.

Security: Implement strong security measures to protect against hacking, fraud, and other cyber threats. This includes using encryption, firewalls, and other security technologies, as well as establishing policies and procedures for data protection and privacy.

Operational Risks: Develop contingency plans for operational disruptions, such as system outages, power failures, or natural disasters, to ensure continuity of service for donors and project organizers.

Financial Risks: Monitor and manage financial risks associated with the platform, such as credit risk, liquidity risk, and market risk. This includes establishing appropriate risk management policies and procedures, setting limits on exposures, and diversifying funding sources.

Reputation: Manage reputation risk by maintaining high

ethical standards, providing clear and transparent information to donors and project organizers, and responding promptly and effectively to any concerns or complaints.

By implementing these risk management strategies, the crowdfunding platform can minimize potential risks and ensure a safe and reliable platform for donors and project organizers.

CONTINGENCY PLAN
FOR UNFORESEEN
EVENTS OR ISSUES

A contingency plan should be developed to address potential unforeseen events or issues that may arise. This plan should include steps for mitigating and resolving issues related to platform functionality, payment processing, and communication with donors and project organizers. It should also include measures to ensure the safety and security of donor information and funds. The contingency plan should be regularly reviewed and updated as necessary to ensure its effectiveness in managing potential risks.

Let's consider a hypothetical contingency plan for the crowdfunding platform:

In the event of unforeseen events or issues that impact the crowdfunding platform, the following contingency plan will be implemented:

Communication: The first step will be to communicate the issue to all stakeholders, including donors, project organizers, and team members. A clear and transparent communication plan will be established to ensure all stakeholders are kept informed throughout the process.

Assessment: A thorough assessment will be conducted to determine the root cause of the issue and to identify potential solutions. This assessment will involve both internal and external experts as necessary.

Plan of Action: Based on the assessment, a plan of action will be developed and communicated to stakeholders. This plan may involve temporary or permanent changes to the platform's features, functionality, or operations.

Implementation: The plan of action will be implemented with a focus on minimizing disruption to the platform's users. This may involve the temporary suspension of certain features or operations until the issue is resolved.

Monitoring and Evaluation: The platform will be closely monitored following the implementation of the plan of action to ensure that the issue has been resolved and that the platform is operating as intended. A thorough evaluation will be conducted to identify any lessons learned and to inform future risk management strategies.

Continual Improvement: The contingency plan will be continually reviewed and updated to ensure that it remains relevant and effective in managing any unforeseen events or issues that may arise in the future.

By implementing this contingency plan, the crowdfunding platform will be able to minimize the impact of unforeseen events or issues on its users and operations, and ensure that the platform continues to function effectively and transparently.

VIII. CONCLUSION

HIGHLIGHTS AND KEY POINTS

In conclusion, the crowdfunding platform outlined in this business plan has the potential to make a significant impact on Sri Lanka's economy and society. By providing a transparent and accessible platform for donors and project organizers, the platform can facilitate the funding of innovative and impactful projects across the country. The key features and functionality of the platform, coupled with a strong marketing and communication strategy and a dedicated team, create a compelling value proposition for potential investors and partners. While there are risks and challenges associated with the platform's development and launch, the risk management strategy and contingency plan are designed to mitigate these risks and ensure the platform's success. We encourage interested investors and partners to support the platform's development and launch, and we are confident that together we can make a positive impact on Sri Lanka's future.

KEYWORDS

- Sri Lanka economic development
- Investment opportunities in Sri Lanka
- Economic revitalization strategies
- Sri Lankan business landscape
- Foreign direct investment in Sri Lanka
- Sri Lanka's economic future
- Government policies for economic growth in Sri Lanka

CITATIONS

"Sri Lanka: A Country Study" by Federal Research Division (Library of Congress)

"Sri Lanka's Development Journey: Issues, Challenges and Prospects" by Institute of Policy Studies of Sri Lanka

"Sri Lanka Economic Summit 2021" by Ceylon Chamber of Commerce

"Repositioning Sri Lanka in the Global Value Chain" by World Bank Group

"Sri Lanka: A Re-emerging Market" by Standard Chartered Bank

"Sri Lanka Economic Update" by Asian Development Bank

"Sri Lanka: Creating a Roadmap for Fiscal Consolidation and Growth" by International Monetary Fund

Federal Research Division (Library of Congress). (2010). Sri Lanka: A Country Study. CreateSpace Independent Publishing Platform.

Institute of Policy Studies of Sri Lanka. (2017). Sri Lanka's Development Journey: Issues, Challenges and Prospects. Institute of Policy Studies of Sri Lanka.

Ceylon Chamber of Commerce. (2021). Sri Lanka Economic Summit 2021. Ceylon Chamber of Commerce.

World Bank Group. (2017). Repositioning Sri Lanka in the Global Value Chain. World Bank Group.

Standard Chartered Bank. (2018). Sri Lanka: A Re-emerging Market. Standard Chartered Bank.

Asian Development Bank. (2021). Sri Lanka Economic Update.

Asian Development Bank.

International Monetary Fund. (2016). Sri Lanka: Creating a Roadmap for Fiscal Consolidation and Growth. International Monetary Fund.